W9-BNR-634

The Americans

McDougal Littell

Evanston, Illinois • Boston • Dallas

Correlation to *The Americans*

Correlation to *The Americans: Reconstruction to the 21st Century*

The Benefits of Trade

Trade arises from having more than you need of something that someone else wants. Suppose you have more food than you could possibly eat. However, you need a winter coat. Suppose you know someone else who has an extra coat but no food. You two can trade. You can exchange the extra food for the extra coat. You each benefit by giving up something you had too much of for something you didn't have at all.

The same principle applies to trade between nations. They exchange something they can produce in a surplus for something they lack. A surplus is more than a person—or a nation—needs of an item.

During the Middle Ages, European nations started producing a surplus of goods they could trade. England and Holland, with large numbers of sheep, produced wool. Weavers in Flanders—a region of present-day Belgium—made cloth from that wool. France produced wine, wheat, and wool. Russia supplied furs and lumber products. Northern Italy made manufactured goods. Eastern Europe mined ores and grew wheat. Each area traded goods it had in abundance for products it lacked. Many groups in Europe benefited from this revival of trade, as the chart below shows.

Trade between Europe and Asia also began to increase. Europeans wanted spices and silk, but they could not produce these goods. What they could do was trade for them with nations in Asia, where the goods were produced. The spices and silk the Europeans brought into their countries were *imports*. The goods they sent to Asia were their *exports*.

The Muslims who lived in the Middle East controlled this trade. European merchants and rulers hoped to win control of the trade for themselves. But because the land route was in the hands of the Muslims, Europeans needed another approach. So they explored for a sea route. For example, when Christopher Columbus sailed west from Europe, he was searching for a sea route to Asia. This search for a sea route for trade led to intense competition between nations. Most European nations participated in a worldwide struggle for economic power.

Activity

World trade still thrives. Make a list of five things that your family owns that come from other countries. List each product and where it came from. Bring your list to class and compare it to those of other students. What nations seem to be most involved in trade with the United States?

Groups in Europe That Benefited from Trade Revival	
Group	**Benefit**
Merchants	Merchants made money by selling the goods for more than it cost to obtain and ship them.
Manfacturers	Manufacturers made money from increased sales of export goods.
Farmers	Farmers had more people willing to buy their crops.
Consumers	Consumers were able to enjoy foods and others goods that couldn't be produced locally.
Rulers	Rulers gained money for their treasuries by taxing trade transactions.

Farming in the English Colonies

In colonial times, the great majority of people lived by farming. Most colonists decided to farm because land was plentiful. Also, people did not need a great deal of money to start farming.

In contrast, it was costly to start new industries in the colonies. Few people who came to North America had enough money to undertake that expense. Even in Europe, the vast majority of people farmed for a living. Most of the colonists who came to North America had been farmers in Europe, and they were simply carrying on the work that they knew.

The different colonial regions had different types of farms. Many of the farms in the New England colonies were small. They produced only enough food for the family that owned and worked the farm.

In the Middle Colonies, though, the growing season was longer and the soil was more fertile. As a result, farmers in these colonies could grow cash crops. In other words, they could grow a surplus that they then sold in towns or shipped to Britain or its colonies in return for cash.

In the Southern Colonies, the most important crops were tobacco, cotton, and rice. All three were cash crops. To grow them profitably, Southern planters built large plantations. On these big farms, large workforces of slaves grew the crops.

The chart below shows the major crops grown and the livestock raised on colonial farms. The chart also indicates how these crops and animals were used.

Over time, farming had an impact on the land. It used up the nutrients, making the soil less fertile. Grazing by cattle damaged the land as well. Colonists used manure and animal remains to try to restore nutrients to the soil. They also tried letting a portion of their fields lie fallow—or uncultivated—for a year.

In New England and some coastal regions, though, the process could not be reversed. The soil in these areas was not very rich in nutrients to begin with. In addition, population growth had an impact. As children reached adulthood, family farms were divided into smaller and smaller pieces. Dividing them further would make the farms too small to support a family. For these reasons, colonists—especially in New England—looked for new land farther west.

Activity

Today, fewer than three percent of all Americans work on farms. Those few people raise enough food to feed all Americans and send large amounts of food abroad. Read about American agriculture today. What factors have made it possible for so few people to produce abundant food for all Americans?

Products of Colonial Farms	
Crops	**Livestock**
Corn, squash, beans, fruits, and vegetables grown for food.	Cattle raised as work animals; for milk, butter, and cheese; for meat; and for leather.
Wheat, barley, and rye grown for food and for sale either in local markets or for export.	Sheep raised for wool and meat.
Hay and oats grown to provide feed for farm animals.	Chickens raised for eggs and meat.
Flax grown to make linen for clothing.	Pigs raised for meat and hides.
Tobacco, cotton, and rice grown as export crops.	Horses raised as work animals.

Mercantilism and Colonies

According to the theory of mercantilism, governments wanted to add gold and silver to their treasuries. To get that gold and silver, they hoped to export goods to other countries that were worth more than the products they imported. The other countries would then have to pay them the difference in gold or silver.

Colonies played an important role under mercantilism for several reasons. Colonies were supposed to produce crops that companies in the home country could sell for a profit. They were expected to provide raw materials that could be used by manufacturing companies in the home country. For example, the numerous forests in North America provided lumber for England, which had fewer trees. The colonies also were supposed to provide markets for items manufactured in the home country.

In some cases, colonies could provide the home country with gold and silver. For example, Spain established colonies in Mexico and South America because of the gold and silver in those areas.

These were some of the reasons that colonies were desirable in theory. In actual practice, colonies had both benefits and costs. These advantages and disadvantages are shown in the chart below.

Activity

Suppose you were in charge of the government of a country that had colonies. How would you prevent people in your colonies from trading with other countries? Write your ideas on a piece of paper. Then write down how you think the colonists would react to these actions.

Benefits and Costs of Mercantilism	
Benefits	**Costs**
+ The colony might have gold or silver that could be added directly to the home country's treasury.	− Gold or silver might be costly to obtain and could be captured during transport.
+ The colony could grow food to feed people in the home country or to be traded at a profit to other countries.	− Money was needed to fund armies to protect colonists from native peoples and to prevent other countries from taking control of the colonies.
+ The colony could supply raw materials useful to home-country manufacturers.	− Colonists might begin their own manufacturing companies and compete with home country companies.
+ Colonists would buy manufactured goods produced in the home country.	− Colonists might ship goods to or buy goods from other European countries.
+ By controlling all shipping to and from the colony, the home country could increase the number and skill of its sailors, who would strengthen the country's navy in the event of war.	− If the manufactured goods colonists bought cost more than the food and raw materials they produced, they would not be able to pay for them.

The Impact of British Taxes

Changes in British taxes—required payments to the government—helped bring about the American Revolution. The British began to increase taxes on American colonists after the French and Indian War (1754–1763). The war proved to be long and costly to Britain. Britain had borrowed huge sums of money to cover the costs of this war, as well as other European wars. In 1754, Britain's national debt was about £72 million. (£ is the symbol for a British pound.) By 1763, the debt nearly doubled to more than £132 million (more than $10 billion today).

After the French and Indian War, Britain stationed 10,000 troops in North America. Maintaining these troops added another heavy expense to the British treasury—about £400,000 a year. To raise money, the British Parliament passed the Sugar Act (1764) and the Stamp Act (1765). The Sugar Act and the Stamp Act marked the beginning of a series of laws that forced colonists to ask this question: Did the benefits of belonging to the British empire outweigh the benefits of becoming an independent nation?

The Sugar Act In passing the Sugar Act, Parliament's goal was to collect £100,000 a year. This amount was expected to cover about 20 percent of Britain's military costs in North America. The Sugar Act included a three-pence tax on every gallon of imported molasses from the French West Indies. Molasses was a thick, sugary syrup used in making rum. The act also taxed many other goods, such as indigo, coffee, wine, and silk. From 1766 to 1775, Britain raised about £30,000 a year in revenue.

The Sugar Act struck an economic blow to merchants and ship captains. Many colonists feared Britain was seizing powers, such as the right to tax, from the colonial legislatures.

The Stamp Act The Sugar Act did not solve Britain's financial problems. Its national debt kept increasing. In 1765, Parliament took more drastic measures and passed the Stamp Act. The goal was to raise £60,000 to £100,000 a year.

The Stamp Act was the first time that the colonists directly paid a tax on goods and services. The Stamp Act required colonists to buy specially stamped paper for printed materials, such as legal documents, pamphlets, and newspapers.

British tax stamp used in 1765.
The Granger Collection, New York

The tax affected all free men and women, both rich and poor, in the colonies. Churchgoers had to pay a stamp tax on prayer books. Engaged couples had to pay a stamp tax on their marriage licenses. African-American laborers, craftworkers, small farmers, southern planters, and northern merchants—all paid the stamp tax.

Especially hard-hit were lawyers and publishers. Lawyers had to pay a £10 stamp tax on their law licenses. They also became alarmed about losing clients who had to pay a tax on documents, such as wills, mortgages, and deeds. Many colonial lawyers spoke out against the Stamp Act and embraced the revolutionary cause. Of the 56 men who signed the Declaration of Independence in 1776, 26 were lawyers.

The American Revolution that followed was not fought over the issue of paying taxes. Rather, the Revolution was fought, in part, over Britain's authority to impose taxes.

Activity

The British government passed the Sugar Act and the Stamp Act to pay the expense of keeping troops in North America. If you had been in charge of the British government, what would you have done to raise the needed money? Write your ideas on a piece of paper. Then exchange papers with a partner. Each of you should then write how you think the colonists would have reacted to your partner's plan.

The Value of Land

Economists say that three things are needed to produce goods: resources, labor, and capital (or money). In the late 1700s, the country had growing numbers of people to supply labor. However, it had little capital. It also had shrinking amounts of a vital resource—land.

In the 1700s, towns on the Atlantic coast were becoming crowded. As children became adults, family farms were divided among them. Over time, farms became smaller and smaller. If the trend continued, farms would become too small. They would not be able to produce enough food to support a family. The need for land was great because the economy was based on farming.

Vast stretches of new land were available just beyond the Appalachian Mountains. In the region north of the Ohio River, called the Northwest Territory, much of the land was rich and fertile—ideal for farming. This territory now forms the states of Ohio, Indiana, Michigan, Illinois, Wisconsin, and part of Minnesota.

The government wanted to make sure that the land was settled in an orderly way. After all, if people simply grabbed whatever they wanted, fights could break out. The Northwest Territory might have become a center of violent conflict rather than peaceful settlement.

The Land Ordinance of 1785 created an orderly system for settling that land. The question remained, how would the land be sold? If the parcel sizes were too large, ordinary people could not afford them. Only the wealthy or land speculators could buy the land. Then they would be able to divide the land up into smaller lots and sell those plots at huge profits.

The ordinance divided the territory into townships, each of which was six miles by six miles. (See the diagram below.) Each township was then divided into 36 lots, or sections. Every lot was one mile by one mile, or 640 acres. The government sold each lot for at least $1 per acre. In the following years, the government sold even smaller lots of land so that more people could afford to buy property. And, the ordinance set aside one section in each township for public education.

Because of the Land Ordinance of 1785, common people had a chance to buy land in the Northwest Territory. And it made sure that the process of settling these lands was well-organized and free of conflict. For these reasons, it was one of the most important acts of Congress in the early years of independence.

Activity

Research land issues in your area today. Are people worried about overcrowding and overdevelopment? Is the lack of development more of a concern? What steps is your local government taking to solve these land issues? Prepare a brief report that outlines the problems and solutions being attempted. Include your own view of how workable these solutions are.

1. SECTIONS OF A TOWNSHIP

6	5	4	3	2	1
7	8	9	10	11	12
18	17	16	15	14	13
19	20	21	22	23	24
30	29	28	27	26	25
31	32	33	34	35	36

2. SUBDIVISIONS OF A SECTION

HALF-SECTION
320 ACRES

QUARTER-SECTION
160 ACRES

HALF QUARTER-SECTION
80 ACRES

QUARTER QUARTER-SECTION
40 ACRES

QUARTER QUARTER-SECTION
40 ACRES

Personal Banking

During Washington's presidency, Alexander Hamilton pushed for the creation of a national bank. Such a bank, he thought, would promote economic growth in two ways. First, it would lend money to businesses. Second, it would issue paper money as currency.

Since then, banks have become enormously important in the American economy, and they affect your life in many ways. Have you ever seen someone writing a check at a store or using an automatic teller machine (ATM) to get cash? These are two common ways that people get to the money that they deposit in a bank.

Every day, people make choices that require money. They may decide to buy a car, put a new roof on their home, or send a child to college. Many people borrow the money from a bank to make these purchases. They sign a contract that binds them to repay the loan over a period of time. They promise to make a fixed payment amount each month during that time.

The bank makes money on the loan by charging interest to the borrower. As you can see from the chart below, the higher the interest rate, the more the bank receives for the loan. The bank also makes more money if the loan is for a longer period of time.

Of course, those interest payments are not all profit. The bank uses this money to cover its costs. Those include the wages it pays to employees and the cost of rent and electricity for the bank offices. Another cost is the interest the bank pays to customers who deposit money in the bank.

Banks typically offer depositors several kinds of accounts. Two are most common.

- **Checking accounts:** Customers use these accounts to meet regular monthly expenses and pay bills. They write checks to buy groceries or pay the electric bill. The business that receives the check deposits it in its own bank. The two banks then transfer the funds between the consumer's and the business's accounts.
- **Savings accounts:** Customers use these accounts for money being saved for use later. Banks pay interest on these accounts, so the amount deposited grows over time. This interest is less than the interest they charge for loans, though.

Banking is a competitive business. Some banks charge fees for each check a customer writes; others do not. Some charge fees if depositors do not have a minimum amount of money in an account. Customers can save money by shopping for the best deal.

For example, the chart below shows how you can save money by shopping around for lower interest rates. The chart shows that by obtaining an 8% rate rather than a 10% rate on a $10,000 loan, you will save $936.00—the difference between $11,718.24 and $12,654.24.

Activity

Call a bank in your area or stop by a bank office. Obtain information on the different kinds of checking and savings accounts the bank offers. Find out (a) the minimum amount that can be used to open an account; (b) how much interest is paid, if any; and (c) what fees the bank charges for the account.

Amount borrowed	Interest rate	Number of payments	Monthly payment	Total amount paid	Total amount of interest paid
$10,000	8%	48 months	$244.13	$11,718.24	$1,718.24
$10,000	9%	48 months	$248.85	$11,944.80	$1,944.80
$10,000	10%	48 months	$253.63	$12,654.24	$2,654.24

The Economics of Slavery

Slavery took hold during the colonial period. Slaves worked on the tobacco farms of the Chesapeake and the rice and indigo plantations of Carolina. The Industrial Revolution in England and the North caused cotton to become the most important crop. Rising demand from textile mills in England and the North spurred cotton production in the South.

Cotton was well-suited to plantation farming. Higher profits came from higher yields. But because work was by hand, higher yields required having larger work forces.

Because large plantations were so efficient for growing cotton, the South had many more large farms than the North did. In the South, almost 5 percent of all the farms had 500 acres of land or more. But in the North, only .1 percent of the farms were that large. In the North, most farms were family-owned, and families did not have the workers available to work large farms.

The organization of the work force depended on the size of the plantation. Most slaveowners had fewer than 20 slaves. The owners often worked in their own fields and directed the work of the slaves.

On larger plantations, owners hired overseers to run the work in the fields. Overseers were often young men who hoped to save enough money to buy their own land. Slaves were organized into work groups called gangs. Each gang was assigned a task to do or area to work each day.

Field work began early in the day and generally lasted until sundown. Slaves worked every day except Sunday. Men performed the hard labor of plowing. Women and children did the weeding and joined with the men in harvesting the crop. Slaves worked late into the night at harvest time.

The free labor by slaves and the demand for cotton made cotton-growing extremely profitable. As a result, the output of cotton and the number of slaves in the South grew rapidly from 1820 to 1860, as the accompanying graph shows.

Slave Population, 1820–1860	
Year	Slaves (in thousands)
1820	1,644
1830	2,162
1840	2,642
1850	3,352
1860	4,097

Source: *Historical Statistics of the United States*

From 1820 to 1860, the output of cotton increased almost 12 times. In the same period, the number of slaves more than doubled. That means that the average slave was producing almost five times as much cotton in 1860 as in 1820. This was partly because of inventions like the cotton gin, which speeded up the process of harvesting cotton. But it was also because slaveowners constantly pushed their enslaved laborers to work harder.

Growing cotton brought profits to slaveowners. It also caused problems. Cotton used up the nutrients in the soil. When the soil was no longer productive, plantations were abandoned. For this reason, there was a gradual westward movement of cotton growing. In the 1810s through the 1830s, people moved away from the coastal states. They built plantations in Tennessee, Alabama, and Mississippi. By the 1840s and 1850s, these lands, too, were becoming unproductive. In this period, cotton growing moved to Arkansas and Texas.

Activity

In the 1840s and later, some critics said that slavery was dying out. They said that—along with being unjust—it didn't make economic sense. Based on what you've read, do you agree or disagree? Why?

Growth of the Factory System

The transformation from household and small shop manufacturing to the factory system is considered a turning point in the nation's economic development. The creation of factories allowed producers to make goods cheaply, quickly, and on a mass scale—all of which helped the United States eventually to become a major industrial power. Economists normally define a factory as a place where there is:

1. substantial output of a product made to be sold to a mass market, rather than locally.

2. complex operations carried out in one or more buildings, much of it relying on the use of machines.

3. an assembly of workers trained to perform specific tasks.

The factory system in the United States began with Samuel Slater's textile mill in 1793. Slater was a textile mechanic from England (where the Industrial Revolution had already had spawned the rise of factories) who migrated to Rhode Island and recreated from memory the country's first cotton-spinning machine.

Several years later, Eli Whitney—already known for his invention of the cotton gin—contributed greatly to the growth of factories with his introduction of interchangeable parts. In 1800, Whitney developed a system for making muskets in which a piece from a weapon could replace the same part on any other weapon. With this standardization of parts, intricate items no longer had to be made slowly by skilled artisans, but could be produced quickly by teams of unskilled factory employees.

A number of other factors spurred the growth of factories in America during the early 1800s. They included a wealth of natural resources needed to produce a variety of items as well as a large population from which to draw the necessary labor force. The nation was also home to an abundance of rivers, which provided the waterpower for the running of many early factories. Playing an equally important role was the War of 1812. The conflict with the British disrupted U.S. trade abroad and forced the country to begin manufacturing many of the products that it had imported before the war.

The factory system developed first in the cotton industry. By 1840 there were 1,200 cotton factories in the United States, most of them in New England. Wool manufacturing was the next industry to adopt the factory system on a large scale. By 1850 some 1,500 woolen mills dotted the landscape of the North, and on the eve of the Civil War the largest textile factories in the country were woolen factories.

The factories of the early and mid-1800s, however, were hardly the size of the giant mills that exist today. While a few cotton factories employed as many as 1,000 workers, most were much smaller. The average cotton mill, for example, had about 60 workers in 1840 and around 110 by 1860.

The growth of factories was mainly a northern phenomenon. With its warm climate and fertile land, the South had emerged as a largely farming society whose economy ran on the production of cash crops such as tobacco, rice, and indigo. And with the invention of the cotton gin in 1793—which prompted a boom in the region's most profitable crop—the South tied its future to agriculture, not manufacturing.

Activity

Chose a factory in your community or state and research its characteristics, including what it produces and how it runs, as well as its history. Based on your research, write a brief report about the factory or draw a detailed image of its operations and present it to the class.

Gold Rush Entrepreneurs

Thousands of fortune seekers came to California in 1849 in the hopes of striking it rich by finding gold. In 1849 alone, 80,000 men came to California in search of a fortune. Towns started up wherever gold was found. Many had colorful names, like Shirt Tail Canyon and You Bet.

The huge jump in population in California created opportunities for entrepreneurs. An entrepreneur is a person who organizes and operates a business. In booming California, there were dozens of opportunities for entrepreneurs to provide services to the gold miners. Levi Strauss became one of the most famous entrepreneurs. He used blue denim and rivets to invent blue jeans— long-lasting pants for the miners. Here are a few other famous entrepreneurs from that era.

- Cornelius Vanderbilt was already wealthy from shipping when the gold rush broke out. He increased his fortune by helping bring the forty-niners to California. His ships carried passengers to the Caribbean coast of Nicaragua in Central America. Then people crossed to the Pacific coast and took one of Vanderbilt's ships to California. The cost per passenger was more than $500.
- Frederick Pope and William Talbot were in the lumber business in Maine. With the building boom caused by the gold rush, they figured that California needed lumber. They sent a shipment of Maine lumber to San Francisco in 1850. When it sold out quickly, they opened a saw mill on Puget Sound, in present-day Washington. Their business thrived for many years.
- Kit Carson, a former fur trapper, lived as a rancher in New Mexico. He recognized that the prospectors would need food. He organized a drive that brought thousands of sheep to California.

- James Phelan came to San Francisco from Cincinnati. He became wealthy selling food to the miners. He used his profits to invest in real estate and became one of San Francisco's first millionaires.
- Mifflin Gibbs was an African American who came to California from Philadelphia. He had success with a San Francisco company that made fine shoes and boots. Eventually, Gibbs left California, however. He was frustrated that, as a black man, he could not enjoy the full rights of a citizen.
- William Fargo and Henry Wells formed Wells, Fargo and Company. They were experienced in carrying packages, mail, and passengers overland in coaches. They won the lucrative government contract to carry mail overland from Missouri to San Francisco. They made even more money by banking.

The few women who ventured to California could also find success as entrepreneurs. Women provided essential services such as cooking and laundry. One woman said, "[California] is the only country I ever was in where a woman received just compensation for work."

Activity

Think about a trend affecting the United States today. Write down the trend. Then write down specific business opportunities that this trend creates. For example, the growth of the computer industry has created the need for stores to sell computer equipment. Develop an idea for a new business—or a variation on a existing business—that meets those needs.

Irish Immigration

One of the largest immigrant groups to the United States in the decades before the Civil War was the Irish. As the graph below shows, immigrants from Ireland equaled about a third of all immigrants in most decades of this period.

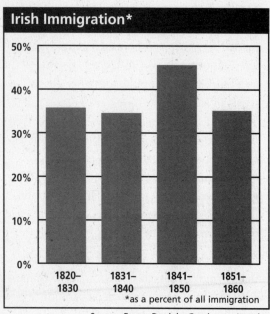

Irish Immigration*

*as a percent of all immigration

Source: Roger Daniels, *Coming to America*

The Irish began to immigrate to the United States in the 1820s because Ireland had too many people for the land to support. Then, beginning in 1846, Irish immigration rose to even higher levels—because of the Great Potato Famine. This tragedy resulted from a crop disease that destroyed potatoes, a staple of the Irish diet. More than 1 million people died because of the resulting famine. To escape, many Irish had no choice but to leave their country.

However, the British did not want the Irish to go to the United States. They preferred the Irish to move to Canada, still a British colony. The British made it easier to go there than to the United States. The Irish could leave on ships for Canada from many Irish ports. To go to the United States, they could only leave from one port in England. In addition, the fare to Canada was less than that for the passage to the United States.

There was more economic opportunity in the United States, however. So the Irish worked around these obstacles. First they went to Canada. After landing there, they took a boat—or walked—to the United States.

Although the United States had more jobs than Canada, those jobs could be hard to come by. Prejudice against the Catholic Irish was strong. Signs advertising jobs often declared, "No Irish Need Apply."

Still, the Irish did find jobs. Men worked mainly as laborers. Thousands of Irish helped to dig the Erie Canal. Thousands more worked on the New Canal built near New Orleans. In 1850, almost two-thirds of all Irish immigrants who lived in Boston worked as laborers or as servants.

Over time, though, the Irish achieved success. It often took two or three generations for immigrant families to climb the economic ladder. By 1880, the majority of Irish in Boston had better jobs than in 1850.

Irish immigration differed from that of the Germans and Scandinavians, who also came in large numbers in the 1800s. Most of the immigrants from those areas came as families. With the Irish, one member of a family often came to the United States alone. That person worked to earn enough to bring another family member. Then the two of them worked, saving until they could bring yet others. This pattern of immigration—called chain migration—is still being followed by other groups today.

Activity

Find out what groups provide most of the immigration today. What patterns do these groups follow? Do they come as families or in chain migration? Why?

The Value of the Border States

The South was at a severe disadvantage as the Civil War began as compared to the North in several key areas. It had fewer people, less industry, and fewer miles of railroad track.

These shortages were one reason that the South was desperate to win the support of the border states. Missouri, Kentucky, Maryland, and Delaware all had sympathy for both the North and the South. These states had close ties to the Northern states. At the same time, they were slave states. As a result, many in the border states agreed with the Southern position on slavery.

The border states also offered the South some strong economic advantages. As the graph below shows, the border states held almost as many people as both the upper South (Virginia, North Carolina, Tennessee, and Arkansas) and the lower South (South Carolina, Georgia, Florida, Mississippi, Alabama, Louisiana, and Texas).

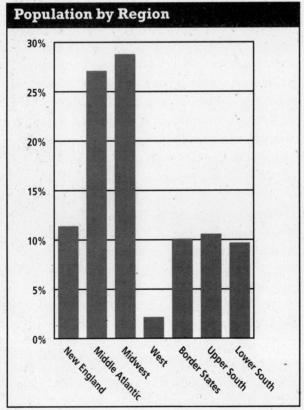

Population by Region

Source: J. G. Randall and David Donald, *The Civil War and Reconstruction*

Adding people from the border states would strengthen the armies of the South—and its ability to produce food. The railroad system of the border states was not well-developed. Still, adding these states would increase Southern rail mileage.

The border states also held two important cities—St. Louis, Missouri, and Baltimore, Maryland. St. Louis was a key port on the Mississippi River. Its population had almost doubled in the prewar decades. Baltimore was almost as busy a port as New Orleans. It handled a thriving trade in both exports and imports. It also had several industries, including textiles and flour milling.

Kentucky was also important economically because the Ohio River ran along its northern border. The Ohio was important because it connected the key states of Pennsylvania, Ohio, Indiana, and Illinois to the Mississippi River.

Along with their economic importance, the border states had strategic value. If the South could gain control of these states, its armies could be ready to attack Northern states from Iowa to New Jersey. Having Missouri would strengthen the South's hold on the Mississippi River. Having Maryland would mean that the Northern capital, Washington, D.C., was surrounded by Southern soil.

While the South hoped to win the border states to its cause, the North was equally determined not to let them go. Northern strategy early in the war aimed at making sure that the border states stayed within the Union.

Activity

What regional economic differences are there in the United States today? Choose one of the following regions: Northeast, Southeast, Midwest, Southwest, West, and Pacific states. Find out what economic activities are carried out in that region. Make a poster or other display to present your findings to the class.

Understanding the Business Cycle

Anational economy goes through periods of good and bad performance. Taken together, these periods are called the "business cycle."

In good times, the economy grows. Businesses produce more goods and services. Consumers buy more, which convinces businesses to produce even more. Wages go up, and so do profits.

In bad times, businesses cut back on production. Instead of hiring workers, they lay workers off. With less money, consumers spend less. Eventually, the economy stops growing. That is, the total value of goods and services produced in the country does not increase from one month to the next. If this happens six months in a row, economists say that the economy is in a recession. If the lack of growth lasts longer and goes deeper, it is called a depression. You can follow this pattern on the graph shown here.

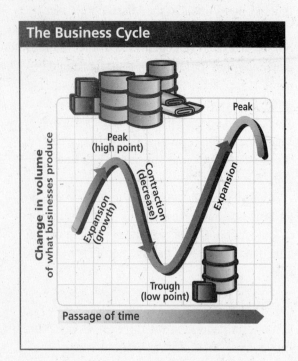

The Business Cycle

Peak

Peak (high point)

Contraction (decrease)

Expansion (growth)

Expansion

Trough (low point)

Change in volume of what businesses produce

Passage of time

Two factors affect the business cycle:

• **Purchases:** Increased spending leads to growth. Less spending means no growth. Consumer spending has this effect. So does spending by the government.

• **Interest rates:** Banks can help growth by lowering interest rates on loans. If loans cost less than before, businesses and consumers are more likely to borrow money. Higher interest rates slow growth down. As interest rates go up, businesses and consumers borrow less money.

During Reconstruction, the United States went through the worst depression that it had experienced up to that time. The depression started with the Panic of 1873. What caused this panic? During and after the Civil War, there was a great boom in railroad building. Most of that building was funded by loans. Serious problems lurked beneath the surface, though.

First, railroads and other businesses borrowed far more money than was healthy for the size of the American economy at the time. Second, there was no government regulation of industry. Business owners pursued profits in any way possible.

These factors, along with financial problems in Europe, combined to cause chaos in late 1873. A major New York financial company was having problems that year. It bought millions of dollars of bonds from a railroad company. (A company issues bonds to borrow money.) When the financial company could not resell the bonds, it collapsed. Loans came due, and businesses were unable to pay them.

The depression that resulted lasted for six years. Thousands of businesses went bankrupt, and many banks closed. Millions of Americans lost their jobs. Farm prices fell. With little income, workers and farmers cut back on spending. This slowed business production even more.

Activity

Today, a governmental body called the Federal Reserve Board has a major influence on the interest rates that banks charge for loans. Find out what that influence is and report to the class. How can the "Fed," as the board is called, affect the economy?

The Law of Supply and Demand

In the 1870s, American farmers became more efficient and produced more food than ever. But much to their disappointment, they didn't make any more money because food prices fell. They were seeing firsthand the economic law of supply and demand.

In free markets, without government controls, supply and demand work together to set prices. According to the law of supply, producers are willing to produce more of a good if the price is higher. That's because they will make more money from selling the good. They want to produce less of the good if the price is lower.

Consumer demand works in the opposite way. Consumers are willing to buy more of a good if the price is lower. If the price increases, they buy less.

The graph below shows how supply and demand come together to set the price of a good. This price is called the "equilibrium price" because it is the point at which supply and demand are equal. At this point, consumers are willing to buy exactly as much output as producers are willing to make.

Several factors affect price-setting:

- **Competition:** If there is only one supplier of a good, consumers have no choice. The supplier has more freedom to set a high price. If a supplier has no competition, it has a *monopoly*.

- **Substitute goods:** If a good is one-of-a-kind, its value is higher. The supplier who has a unique good can charge more. But if consumers can find a substitute for the good, then the good is no longer one-of-a-kind. As a result, the price of the good may fall.

- **Government action:** Some goods are in limited supply. In a free market, the suppliers of those limited goods can increase the price to very high levels because demand will always be greater than supply. In these cases, the government may decide to put limits on the suppliers' ability to set prices. It may, for instance, establish prices.

Activity

How do the salary negotiations between sports teams and professional athletes show the laws of supply and demand? Suppose the athlete is the best player at a particular position? What effect will that have on the athlete's salary? What principle of price setting is at work? Suppose the athlete is a free agent who can sign with any team. What effect will that have on the athlete's salary? What principle of price setting does this demonstrate?

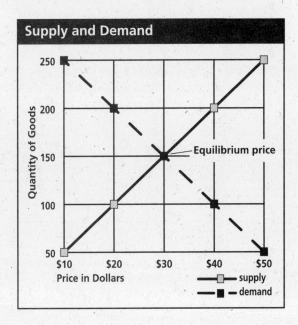

The Union Struggle

After the Civil War, labor unions began to form national organizations to win improvements for workers. The Knights of Labor included workers from different trades. This union grew rapidly from the early 1870s until 1886. The Knights lost public support because of the Haymarket Riot and other labor conflicts that year.

During the same year, 1886, Samuel Gompers, a leader of the cigar makers' union, helped to found the American Federation of Labor. The AFL was very different from the Knights, as the chart below shows.

The two unions had different goals. The Knights wanted major changes in the economy. Leader Terence Powderly said that workers, by uniting, could "own and operate mines, factories, and railroads." Gompers, the head of the AFL, dismissed Powderly and other Knights leaders as dreamers. When asked what he wanted for his union members, he answered simply, "More." By this, he meant more time off and more wages.

The Knights were weakened by a lack of practical organizing skills among Powderly and other leaders. These leaders were also unable to control local groups. Gompers, by contrast, was a strong leader. His focus on bread-and-butter issues appealed to union members. Still, while the AFL did survive, it was never very powerful in the 19th century. It was weakened by the decision not to include unskilled industrial workers. These workers were a growing percentage of the work force.

There were other reasons that the unions did not grow very strong. First, they were able to organize only a small fraction of American workers. They did not have enough members to push business owners to change. Second, those business owners had too much money and power to bend to union demands. Third, the government tended to support the corporations and not the unions. It would take many decades before union power would grow.

Activity

Research a union that is active today. Find out when the union began and how it changed over time. Find out how many members it has now, what regions of the country it is strongest in, and what major issues it campaigns for. Present your findings in a report or a poster.

Knights of Labor	American Federation of Labor (AFL)
Recruited individual workers.	Pulled together unions that had already been formed.
Recruited workers regardless of skill levels or industry; even included farmers.	Tried to unionize only workers who were skilled.
Recruited women workers.	Did not seek to include women, even if they were skilled workers.
Opposed using strikes or collective bargaining to gain results.	Relied on collective bargaining to improve conditions. Used strikes to win better contracts.
Had a larger treasury than AFL.	Member unions raised insurance and strike funds to give workers resources in event of a strike.

Conflict over Tariffs

Tariffs are taxes added to the cost of goods imported from another country. The importer is responsible for paying the tax, known as a customs duty. To offset this fee, importers normally must raise prices on their goods, thus making it more difficult to sell them abroad.

Tariffs have two main purposes. One is to raise revenues for the federal government. From 1789 until the 1860s, tariffs were the major source of revenue for the federal government. The other goal of tariffs is to protect a nation's industries by making it harder for foreign competitors to import their goods. The government used tariffs in the early 1800s to encourage American industries to grow. In 1816, for example, textile manufacturers in Lowell, Massachusetts, convinced Congress to place a tariff on cloth imported from such countries as India and Britain.

As helpful as tariffs may have been to the burgeoning American industries, they caused friction between the country's different regions and economic classes. The prominent battles over tariff rates during the Gilded Age were nothing new; this particular economic policy has prompted much debate and disagreement throughout the nation's history.

For instance, while manufacturers in the Northeast praised the Tariff of 1816 for the boost it gave to businesses, residents of the South and West strongly opposed the tax. The people of these regions did not depend on manufacturing for their livelihood, and they resented a tax that increased the price of the numerous imports they purchased.

A tariff passed in 1828 met with even greater outrage from Southerners. The leaders of South Carolina referred to it as the Tariff of Abomination and threatened to secede from the Union if the tax were not repealed. A tense standoff ensued between state and federal leaders, which ended only after Congress passed a compromise bill that gradually lowered the tariff.

By the late 1800s, tariffs had become one the main points of debate between the country's two major political parties. In general, the Democratic Party favored low tariffs, arguing that high import duties helped only wealthy merchants and that freer and more open trade between countries would in the long run raise the standard of living among all people. Republicans, on the other hand, generally advocated higher tariffs. They contended that increased import duties benefited American businesses, which led to more jobs and better pay for American workers.

As a Republican congressman from Ohio, William McKinley was one of the leading proponents of protecting American industry through high tariffs. His tariff bill, known as the McKinley Tariff Act of 1890, raised the tax rate on imports to their highest level yet—almost 50 percent.

Whatever aid it may have provided to the nation's businesses, the McKinley Tariff Act proved disastrous for the Republican Party. The high tariff led to an increase in the price of many consumer items, and angry voters responded by giving Democrats control of the House of Representatives during the congressional elections of 1890. McKinley, however, remained undeterred. When he became U.S. president in 1896—with overwhelming support from the business community—he oversaw the passage of the Dingley Tariff, which raised import duties to their highest rate to date.

Activity

Write several paragraphs arguing in favor of either low or high tariffs. Use information from this page, your textbook, and other resources to support your argument.

The Rise of Department Stores

The 1880s saw a revolution in how goods were sold—the department store. Up until then, Americans had bought what they needed at small general stores or dry-goods stores. These stores had limited choices of clothing, furniture, and household items.

But as more people moved into cities, a few ambitious merchants opened much larger stores in the cities' downtown districts. These were called department stores because they had different departments, such as women's wear, men's wear, and furniture. Some of the earliest department stores were Macy's in New York, John Wanamaker in Philadelphia, and Marshall Field's in Chicago.

Department stores succeeded largely because they were able to buy large volumes of goods for low prices. As a result, they were able to sell quality goods to consumers for reasonable prices. They also sold an incredible variety of goods, from luggage to children's toys.

If a customer was dissatisfied with a good, he or she could exchange it. The stores offered fixed prices and year-end sales that provided even bigger bargains. Sales clerks were trained to give customers personal service. Marshall Field's motto was, "Give the lady what she wants."

The department stores themselves resembled rich and luxurious palaces. They had marble stairs, beautiful lighting, and expensive carpeting. Fine wood paneling lined the walls. Everything was planned to make the customers feel special.

The stores were extremely successful. By 1900, every American city had one—and often two—large department stores. The stores changed how Americans shopped. The small general store faded away, except in rural areas. The chart below shows important ways in which department stores were different from small general stores.

Activity

What goods and services do department stores offer today? What other ways of selling compete with department stores?

General Stores or Dry-Goods Stores	Department Stores
In small towns	In large cities
Small—a few rooms	Large, multistory buildings
Single owner who works in store along with clerks	Owners form corporation and act as managers
A few sales clerks, usually males	Thousands of sales clerks, usually females
Usually only one store	Begin with one store but grow to include a chain of several
Earn profits by marking up goods as much as demand allows	Earn profits by buying goods in large quantities and selling a high volume at low markup
Merchandise—bolts of cloth, sewing needs, shoes and gloves, some household goods	Merchandise—ready-made clothing, jewelry, toys, furniture, household items
Prices not labeled; clerk and customer haggled over price	Goods clearly marked with price; no haggling
Returns not allowed	Money sometimes returned if customer not satisfied
No advertising	Newspaper ads and handbills

Tariffs and Taxes

In 1913, Congress passed the first income tax. The law put into effect the tax that had been authorized by the Sixteenth Amendment. However, the new tax measure was actually not the main focus of congressional attention. The tax measure was just a part of another new law—a major overhaul of the nation's tariff system.

The Underwood–Simmons Tariff Act of 1913 was the result of decades of efforts by Democratic party leaders to cut the tariff. The act cut tariffs on nearly 1,000 goods. Progressive Democrats liked the law because tariffs were lifted on most food and clothing—essential items for Americans struggling to make ends meet. The new law meant that consumer goods would be cheaper. The new tariff measure cut the tariffs from 40 percent to 29 percent.

The new tariffs had a disadvantage, however. The cuts reduced federal income from customs duties by $100 million. How would this money be replaced? That is where the income tax came in. The first federal income tax was added to Underwood's tariff bill to provide a new source of revenue for the government.

The tax applied only to income over $3,000 per year ($4,000 for married couples). As people earned more, the tax rate went up. The higher the income, the higher the rate. The rate went from 1% up to a maximum of 7%. Progressives liked this idea because it seemed fair to poor people.

The tax applied not only to individual income but also to corporate income. This way the Progressives could tap into the mounting profits of the country's growing businesses.

As the graph shows, between 1911 and 1920, the share of federal income from taxes grew larger and larger. Meanwhile—as the backers of the new tariff law expected—the share of tariff revenues dropped sharply.

Activity

Find out where different levels of government get their money today. Look into revenues for federal, state, and local government. How does the source of money differ for these three levels?

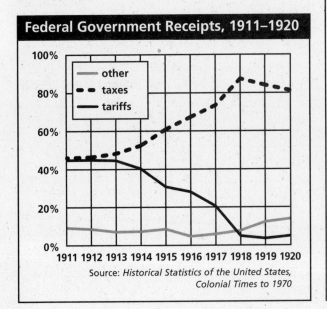

Federal Government Receipts, 1911–1920

- other
- taxes
- tariffs

100% 80% 60% 40% 20% 0%

1911 1912 1913 1914 1915 1916 1917 1918 1919 1920

Source: *Historical Statistics of the United States, Colonial Times to 1970*

The Economic Causes of Imperialism

In the late 1800s, European powers followed a policy of imperialism. In imperialism, a strong country takes over the political, economic, or social life of a weaker nation. Great Britain, France, Germany, Belgium, and other European nations acquired weaker countries as colonies throughout Asia and Africa.

European nations wanted colonies for economic reasons. For example, Great Britain is an island nation with few natural resources. It acquired colonies to supply raw materials for its factories. British companies took raw materials like Egyptian cotton and West African palm oil. Then they exported the finished products—cotton cloth and oil-based candles and soap—around the world.

Americans wanted to get into the act, too. Senator Albert J. Beveridge of Indiana summed up the economic argument for imperialism at the end of the 1800s. "Today," he said, "we are raising more [crops] than we can consume. Today, we are making more than we can use. Therefore, we must find new markets for our produce, new occupation for our capital, new work for our labor." All parts of society, he argued, would benefit if the United States had colonies.

Unlike the European powers, the United States acquired few colonies. But it found a number of ways to gain influence in other countries without actually making them colonies.

The Hawaiian Islands were a good example of how U.S. influence grew. Since the early 1800s, Americans had migrated to Hawaii and become planters there. One of their major crops was sugar. Many of the American planters grew wealthy and gained influence over Hawaii's government.

The Hawaiian planters had an economic advantage over sugar growers in other parts of the world. They could ship their sugar to the United States without paying any tariffs. But this advantage disappeared in 1891. That year, Congress ended tariffs on sugar from all countries in the world. In addition, it gave U.S. sugar growers a government subsidy—payments to encourage them to grow sugar.

The sugar growers in Hawaii were outraged. Because Hawaii was not part of the United States, they did not receive the subsidy. So, in the hope of having the United States take over Hawaii, they staged a revolt against the native Hawaiian ruler, Queen Liliuokalani. The planters established their own government and asked the United States to annex Hawaii. However, President Grover Cleveland refused to approve the annexation. In 1900, though, at the end of the Spanish-American War, Hawaii became a territory of the United States.

In a variety of ways, the United States expanded its influence in other nations. Puerto Rico and the Philippines became territories of the United States. Although Cuba became independent after the Spanish-American War, the U.S. government had a strong influence on the Cuban government. The United States supported a revolution in Panama and then negotiated the right to build the Panama Canal, providing a shortcut between the Atlantic Ocean and the Pacific Ocean.

In all these cases, American economic motives were central. The American government helped to protect American corporations in several Latin American countries. And the Panama Canal helped to spur American trade and shipping with the world.

Activity

Do research to find out what the relationship is today between the United States and one of these countries: Puerto Rico, Cuba, the Philippines, or Panama. How much trade is there between the two countries? If trade is carried on, what goods are traded? If no trade is carried on, why not?

Russian Communism

The Russian Revolution brought about the first Communist government in the world. Communism was based on the writings of the 19th century German philosophers and economists Karl Marx and Friedrich Engels. They were outraged by the problems caused by the Industrial Revolution in Europe.

Marx and Engels believed that private ownership of property was the problem. They said that all people in a society should own property together. Society would distribute goods to people as they needed them. No longer would there be rich and poor. Marx and Engels described their ideal society in a book called *The Communist Manifesto* (1848). They argued that while the development of a Communist society was bound to happen, it would not happen peacefully. Instead, the workers must seize power in a revolution.

In Russia in the early 1900s, the Communists gained a great following, partly because of the poor conditions in which peasants and workers lived. Vladimir I. Lenin, a Russian who had been greatly influenced by Marx, became leader of one group of Communists, the Bolsheviks.

In 1917, during the chaos of World War I, Lenin saw a chance for the Bolsheviks to seize power. In the fall of that year, he led a revolution against the provisional government that had come to power after the fall of the government of Czar Nicholas II in March, 1917. A civil war followed, which the Bolsheviks won in 1922. In 1922, the Communists renamed the country the Union of Soviet Socialist Republics (USSR). Russia became one of several communist republics in the new Soviet Union.

Once in power, the Communists made enormous changes in the country's economy. They seized land from large landholders and distributed it to peasants. They gave great control of factories to workers. Government planners decided what products a factory should produce, how the products should be made, and what prices should be charged. The government chose the workers, assigned them jobs, and decided what their working hours were.

The Soviet government was brutal in its treatment of peasants. Starting in 1928, the government seized control of more than 25 million farms in the USSR. It combined them into collective farms.

And although communism preached equality, Soviet society was hardly equal. Members of the Communist party enjoyed privileges that others did not. The government also exercised tight control of politics and the media. People who spoke against the government could be killed or imprisoned.

The Soviet government did succeed in turning the Soviet Union into an industrial nation. The production of steel, coal, oil, and electricity all increased. But to achieve these goals, the government limited production of goods that people needed, like food, housing, and clothing.

By the 1970s and 1980s, the Russian people were becoming more dissatisfied with their lives and with their government. In 1985, a new Soviet leader, Mikhail Gorbachev, came to power. He tried to bring more freedom into the Soviet system. His reform efforts touched off a wide-spread independence movement, as the various republics under Soviet rule rose up and challenged their communist regimes. In 1991, Gorbachev resigned as head of the government, and the Soviet Union ceased to exist. The republics that had once comprised the USSR–including Russia–became free and independent nations.

Since 1991, Russia has struggled in its transition from a communist to a capitalist economy. The Russian people can now start businesses and own property. But with much of Russian society plagued by high unemployment and poverty, progress toward prosperity had been slow.

Activity

After World War II, several nations became Communist. These included China, North Vietnam, North Korea, Cuba, and several countries in Eastern Europe. Find out what happened to the Communist system in one of these countries and report to the class.

Understanding the Stock Market

One of the symbols of prosperity in the 1920s was the booming stock market. Corporations issue stock to raise money. A corporation declares its aim to offer a certain number of shares of stock for sale. An investment bank arranges to have the shares sold. People who think that the value of the shares will increase over time buy them. The money the buyers pay—minus a percentage that the bank keeps—goes to the corporation.

Corporations issue stock for various reasons. They may need money to expand into a new line of business. They may want to buy another company.

Each person who buys a share of stock owns a piece of the corporation. These stockholders have certain rights. They have the right to receive information about the corporation's finances. They can attend stockholder meetings and vote for people to serve on the company's board of directors. They also receive dividends. When the corporation earns profits, its directors declare a dividend. This is a sum of money paid on each share of stock owned. The corporation sends dividend checks to each and every stockholder.

Stockholders benefit from owning stocks in two ways. First, they receive dividends. Second, they gain if the value of the stock goes up. Shares of stock in thousands of corporations are traded every day. The value of each share can go up or down. Sometimes factors such as the overall health of the economy or government actions affect the price of a share. The performance of the corporation itself has a big impact on its stock price. If a company's profits are increasing and its managers are competent, investors will usually bid up the value of that stock. If a company is having hard times or losing out to competitors, its stock price will fall.

In the 1920s, stock prices rose steadily. From May 1928 to September 1929, the average stock price soared by 40 percent.

Because stock prices were rising, many people began to buy shares. By 1929, about 4 million Americans owned stock. Stock brokers made it easy for people to own shares. Brokers allowed people to buy on credit (borrowed money). Buyers only had to pay 25 percent of the stock price in cash. The other 75 percent they could owe. Buyers typically planned to pay it back in the future, when they sold the shares at a higher price. If the stock price fell, though, these buyers would be in trouble. They would have to pay back the money that they borrowed, even though the stock was no longer worth as much.

This process was called "margin buying." It was hugely popular during the stock market boom of the late 1920s.

Then, on October 28 and 29, 1929, stock prices fell dramatically. The Dow Jones Industrial Average lost nearly one-fourth of its value in October 1929.

By the middle of November, investors had lost $30 billion in the stock market. Investors who had bought stocks on credit could not pay back their loans. In turn, many stockbrokers and banks went bankrupt because they could not collect back the money they had lent to investors. This stock market crash helped to cause the Great Depression, which lasted from 1929 until World War II.

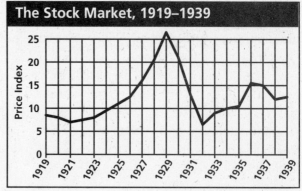

The Stock Market, 1919–1939

Source: *Historical Statistics of the United States, Colonial Times to 1970*

Activity

The New York Stock Exchange handles the buying and selling of the most shares of stock in the world. Each day, news outlets report how stocks did—on average—by looking at the Dow Jones Industrial Average. Find out what that average is, how it is computed, and what it tells investors.

Women's Economic Impact

The strides that women made during the 1920s included notable advances on the economic front. During the Roaring Twenties, women became a greater presence in the nation's labor force as the number of female workers increased throughout the decade. It was away from the office, however, that women appeared to make their greatest impact on the economy. During the 1920s women emerged as the main purchasers in society—which increased their importance in the country's growing consumer culture and made them vital to the nation's economic growth.

With the end of World War I—and the return home of thousands of fighting men—many women lost the jobs they had held during the labor-scarce war years. Nonetheless, the number of women working in the decade after the war actually increased. Emboldened by a new sense of political and social freedom, women in the 1920s sought greater economic independence as well. Between 1920 and 1930, the number of working women rose from almost 8.6 million to nearly 10.8 million—a figure that represented about 22 percent of the country's workforce.

Despite this increase in numbers, however, the gains made by women in the workplace were limited. Women's wages lagged behind those of men throughout the 1920s—as they have all the way through the present-day. In addition, women in the twenties were discouraged from seeking employment in all but a small number of fields. During the 1920s, 86 percent of all working women could be found in but a mere 10 occupations, most of them low paying jobs such as housekeeper, salesperson, and clerical worker. Throughout the decade, the percentage of working women who were lawyers remained at about 3 percent, while the percentage of the female labor force made up of doctors actually dipped from 5 percent in 1920 to slightly more than 4 percent in 1930.

It was thus in another role that the twenties woman made her greatest contribution to the nation's economy: that of consumer. By the 1920s, it had become clear that women were the major buyers of goods in society. The numbers certainly bore this out. During the decade, women spent more than two-thirds of the roughly $47 billion expended each year on consumer goods. Statistics from the era also showed that women made more than 80 percent of all purchases at department stores and grocery shops. What's more, they spent more on clothes than any other member of their family. A magazine article in 1929 summed up the situation with the title "The Home Woman as Buyer and Controller of Consumption."

The buying power of women certainly drew the attention of corporate America. Businesses competed to put out the latest item to attract women while advertisers catered to their various needs and desires. Entire industries even arose around women and their spending dollars. Between 1920 and 1930, for example, the number of beauty shops in the country swelled from 5,000 to 40,000. Meanwhile, the sale of cosmetics grew from $17 million before World War I to $141 million by 1925.

In their role as the nation's main consumers, women became an important part of the U.S. economy, which relies on the continual buying and selling of goods in order to remain strong. Thus, as the twenties ended, women had begun to make their mark on the country's economic landscape.

Activity

Research a particular issue surrounding women in the workplace today and write a brief report on it. Possible topics include pay disparities between men and women, advances in the legal and medical professions, or a look at the so-called "glass ceiling." Use the Internet and other library resources to aid you in your research.

The Great Depression

The Great Depression that began in 1929 was the longest, deepest period of hard times in American history. The two graphs below show how much unemployment and business failures rose during the Depression. Six factors helped make this depression the worst of all.

- **The gold standard:** In the 1920s, paper money was backed by gold. Governments pledged to exchange gold for paper money if a person wanted it. This meant that a government could only print as much money as equaled the value of the gold it held. Several years after the Great Depression began, nations—including the United States—dropped the gold standard.

- **The business cycle:** Government and business leaders saw depressions as natural parts of the business cycle. They knew that people would lose their jobs and wages would fall in a depression. However, they believed that eventually businesses would hire more workers because labor was cheaper. Then production would increase, and the economy would grow again.

- **The makeup of the economy:** In 1929, farm products and raw materials formed a big share of the American economy. When prices on these goods fell, trade around the world slowed down. The slowdown in trade spread the Great Depression worldwide.

- **Economic weakness in Europe:** Several nations in Europe had shaky economies in the 1920s. The collapse of American demand for their goods hit these countries hard. Later, the United States raised tariff rates. The aim was to protect the nation's hard-hit industries from cheap imports. But several other nations raised their own tariffs. The result was to further weaken world trade.

- **A drop in consumer spending:** As crop prices fell, farmers had to cut back on spending. They simply didn't have the money to buy goods.

Investors who had lost money in the Great Crash also did not have money to spend. As unemployment rose and wages dropped, factory and office workers faced the same problems. Consumers had to cut back to buying just essential items—food and clothing.

- **A credit crunch:** Consumers feared the future. They stopped buying goods on credit (borrowed money). This caused problems for automakers and other businesses that made expensive products. At the same time, falling incomes and failing businesses hurt banks. Consumers and companies were unable to repay their loans. Banks became more cautious about issuing new loans.

The nation did not recover from the Great Depression until World War II. When the United States entered World War II, the federal government greatly increased its spending for arms. American companies hired more workers, and the economy finally improved.

Activity

The Great Depression was a worldwide economic crisis. Choose one other country in the world. Find out what impact the Depression had on that country. Report your findings to the class.

Source: *Historical Statistics of the United States, Colonial Times to 1970*

Deficit Spending

Deficit spending is the act by which the federal government spends more money than it receives in revenue. In general the government engages in deficit spending during economic slowdowns as a way of pumping money into the economy to stimulate business activity and job growth.

Before the 1930s, most presidential administrations were reluctant to engage in deficit spending. The reasons were twofold. First, deficit spending increases the national debt, or the overall amount of money the United States owes to its creditors such as banks, corporations, as well as foreign governments and even private individuals. Too large a debt can become a great burden by making it difficult for the government to borrow money. It also requires the government to divert funds away from various programs each year in order to pay back the money it owes.

Secondly, most economic and political leaders believed that the best way to manage the economy was through a laissez-faire, or "hands off" approach. Conventional wisdom taught that there was no need for the government to try to spur economic growth—when left alone, a capitalist system naturally created a thriving economy and near full employment.

The Great Depression, of course, changed all this. As the financial catastrophe of the 1930s worsened with each passing year, leading economists were at a loss to explain why the nation's economy could not right itself.

It was during this time that British economist John Maynard Keynes stepped forward and claimed that the classical economists had it all wrong. In what became his landmark book, *The General Theory of Employment, Interest, and Money* (1936), Keynes argued that the normal workings of an economy did not necessarily bring full employment and stability and that government intervention, in the form of deficit spending and other measures, was the key to alleviating economic downturns.

President Franklin Roosevelt practiced deficit spending in an effort to stimulate job growth. The benefits of deficit spending, however, did not become apparent—and the Great Depression did not end—until the onset of World War II, when the government greatly increased its expenditures and unemployment all but disappeared.

In the years that followed, the nation's political leaders became strong proponents of deficit spending—and not just during times of financial or military crisis. Keynesian philosophy became official policy with the Employment Act of 1946, which gave the federal government greater authority in trying to maintain full employment and economic growth.

The Keynesian technique reached a peak in the 1960s, when a large tax cut coupled with great amounts of government spending spurred a decade-long economic boom. The situation turned dramatically, however, in the 1970s when a new phenomenon known as "stagflation"—high inflation coupled with high unemployment—crippled the U.S. economy. This time it was the Keynesians who were stumped, as government intervention seemed to provide little help. When Washington, D.C. pumped money into the economy to create jobs, inflation increased; when it tightened the money supply to curb inflation, unemployment rose.

It was during the 1970s that a number of leading economists began to voice opposition to Keynesian economics and called for less government influence in the economy. Thirty years later, the debate seems far from settled. The merits of deficit spending as well as the larger issue of how much the federal government should intervene in the economy continue to prompt disagreement in economic and political circles—and probably will for years to come.

Activity

Work with a partner to track the nation's deficits and debt from 1990 through today. Based on your research, write a brief report on the subject or draw a detailed graph or chart depicting the information you found.

The Lend-Lease Act

As Congress debated the passage of the Lend-Lease bill, British official H. Duncan Hall summarized what the measure meant to Great Britain. "For the first time in its history the United Kingdom waited anxiously on the passage of an American law, knowing that its destiny might hang on the outcome."

The Lend-Lease plan was indeed viewed by many Britons as all that stood between their survival and defeat in 1941. With much of Western Europe conquered by then, the British faced the Axis powers all alone—and with little money to mount a fight. "Britain's broke," British ambassador Lord Lothian told the American press in late 1940.

Strangely enough, few Americans—including even Franklin Roosevelt—believed at first that Britain could be in such dire financial straits. After all, the British were still rulers of a large and far-flung empire. Holdings such as India and Suez Canal, however, did not necessarily translate into cash, and it was only after British Prime Minister Winston Churchill handed over Britain's accounting records to U.S. officials did they realize how much help the British needed.

It was not long after this that the Roosevelt administration developed the idea to in essence lend military equipment and other forms of aid to Britain and the other countries aligned against the Axis powers.

The Lend-Lease measure won passage despite intense and vocal opposition from isolationists, who viewed the plan as a significant step toward American involvement in the war. In one of the more famous attacks, Montana Senator Burton K. Wheeler called the bill "the New Deal's triple A foreign policy; it will plow under every fourth American boy." Roosevelt referred to the remark "as the most dastardly, unpatriotic thing . . . that has been said in public life in my generation."

The Lend-Lease program, which lasted through the end of the war, handed out nearly $50 billion in aid to some 38 countries. Great Britain—which included the United Kingdom, Australia, New Zealand, and South Africa—received the largest amount of assistance, with $31,392,361,000. The Soviet Union was second with $11,297,833,000.

The largest portion of the aid—about 49 percent—consisted of munitions, from weapons to airplanes and tanks. About 21 percent came in the form of industrial materials and parts, 14 percent in agricultural products, 5 percent in petroleum products, and 11 percent in miscellaneous services.

The Lend-Lease program proved most beneficial to the Allied military effort, with Prime Minister Churchill once referring to it as "Hitler's death warrant." The plan, however, turned out to be a less than ideal economic measure for America. In the end, only about $10 billion in loans were repaid to the United States. Britain, which had little money by 1945, was asked to repay only $650 million. Belgium was the only country to pay back the United States ($191,215,983) more than it received ($148,394,457).

Activity

Do further research on the debate in Congress over the Lend-Lease bill and write a brief narrative of the episode using quotes from various political leaders on each side of the argument.

The Growing Economic Role of Government

During the New Deal and World War II, the federal government played a larger role in the American economy. New Deal programs cost money. Social Security payments added to government spending as well. The effect on the federal budget can be seen by looking at federal spending over the period. From 1925 until 1931, the federal government never spent more than $3.6 billion. In 1934—as New Deal spending took effect—that number shot up to $6.7 billion. It continued to climb until it reached $9.6 billion in 1940.

Conservative critics charged that President Franklin D. Roosevelt was trying to turn the United States into a socialist country. The newspapers owned by William Randolph Hearst referred to "the Red New Deal with a Soviet seal endorsed with a Moscow hand."

Government spending soared even higher during World War II because the government was buying armaments and paying millions of people in the armed forces. The government increased its spending in 1941 to $14 billion. By 1945, spending had skyrocketed to $95.2 billion. There were few complaints about this level of spending during the war, however, because the nation was fighting for its survival.

With the New Deal and the war, the federal government played a growing role in the nation's economy. The government was bigger and had more workers. Even after the war ended, defense spending stayed high because of the Cold War.

The true impact of the New Deal and the war on the role of the federal government is clear when looking at federal spending after the war. In 1946, spending began to drop, reaching a postwar low of $36.5 billion in 1948. This level was much lower than during World War II. Still, it was more than 10 times the amount spent before the New Deal. The government would never again be as small as it had been in the 1920s.

Activity

Find out how much the federal government spent in a recent year. Find out what proportion of that spending went to different areas, such as defense, social welfare, administration, interest on federal debt, and others. Draw a pie graph showing how the money was divided.

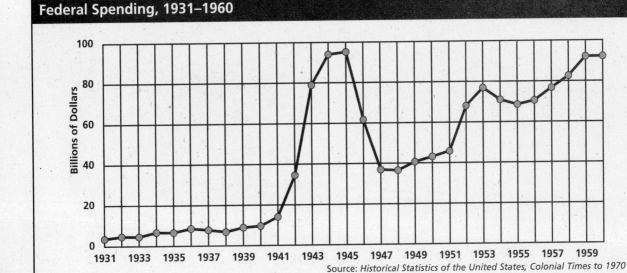

Federal Spending, 1931–1960

Source: *Historical Statistics of the United States, Colonial Times to 1970*

Name _____ Date _____

The Space Race Pays Off

The Cold War twice flared into actual combat—in Korea and Vietnam. During the 1960s, the United States and the Soviet Union met in another conflict. Though peaceful, it was hard fought. It was the space race.

The Soviet Union began this race in 1957 by launching a satellite called *Sputnik*. It was the first human-made object sent out of the earth's atmosphere. The launch stunned Americans because it showed that the Soviets had powerful rockets. These rockets, people feared, could be used to send nuclear weapons to the United States.

The *Sputnik* launch spurred the U.S. government to push harder in its own space program. In 1961, President Kennedy vowed that the United States would land a man on the moon before the decade's end. In 1969, Neil Armstrong and Buzz Aldrin fulfilled that promise.

The space program was popular early in the 1960s. As the years passed, though, many questioned the billions spent to send a man to the moon. Critics said the government should use the money to solve problems on earth. The space program also suffered from mounting criticism of the military over the Vietnam War. Soon after Armstrong's historic walk on the moon, Congress began to cut space funding.

Still, space research continued. One program proved to be of great benefit on earth. In 1972, the National Aeronautics and Space Administration (NASA) launched the first of the satellites that came to be called Landsat. These satellites orbited the earth taking pictures of the planet. They took thousands of pictures of places all over the earth. These pictures could show changes on earth over time. The satellites also made contact with sensors placed on the ground. The data they gathered from the sensors included such information as water temperatures and pollution levels.

The satellite images were an instant hit. Officials, scientists, and economists all over the world have used them in many ways.

- to measure the growth of cities and to identify settlement patterns
- to find the best time to plant crops and to monitor the health of the crops
- to determine the health of forests and to find out how rapidly forests are being cut down
- to identify pollution problems and to measure water quality

In 1998, NASA launched the seventh Landsat satellite. The program was planned to continue into the new millennium. Future missions will gather data for studies of global climate changes. Landsat images have helped government planners around the world. They have also been used by private businesses. One company studied Landsat images to find good spots to locate fast-food restaurants.

Activity

The United States government makes Landsat images available to people all over the world. It charges a fee for the use of the information, but the fee is small. Write an essay stating whether you agree or disagree with this policy. Remember to give reasons and examples to support your argument.

The Soviet satellite *Sputnik I*, launched in 1957.
Sovfoto/Eastfoto.

Measuring the Postwar Boom

Economists measure a country's prosperity by looking at its gross national product. The gross national product (GNP) is the total market value of all goods and services produced by the country during a period of time—usually a year.

In comparing GNP from year to year, economists must be careful. GNP might increase simply because of rising prices—not because of increased production.

Economists avoid this problem by figuring GNP in terms of "constant prices." They choose one year as a benchmark year. Then they compare price levels of other years to that year. If prices were higher because of inflation, they adjust the value of the GNP downward. If prices were generally lower than the benchmark year, they increase the value of that year's GNP. By this method, economists can compare GNP in different years fairly.

The graph below shows GNP of the United States from 1945 to 1960 in terms of constant dollars. From a low of just under $310 billion in 1947, the GNP rose to nearly $490 billion by 1960. That's an overall increase of 60 percent from 1947.

To see how growth affects ordinary people, economists also look at median family income. *Median* means that there are an equal number above and below that point. Economists also adjust these income figures for inflation, just as they do with GNP.

The graph below shows median income from 1947 to 1960 in terms of constant dollars. From a low of $4,349 in 1949, median family income in the United States rose to $6,347. That's an increase of almost 46 percent. This growth in family income shows that Americans enjoyed a rising standard of living after World War II. They could buy more goods and live more comfortably.

U.S. Median Family Income, 1947–1960

Source: *Historical Statistics of the United States, Colonial Times to 1970*

U.S. Gross National Product, 1945–1960

Source: *Historical Statistics of the United States, Colonial Times to 1970*

Activity

Look at either the GNP or the median family income of the United States over ten recent years. Be sure to use figures reflecting constant dollars. Make a graph showing the changes over this period. Is the economic measure going up or down? What trends does this suggest?

Poverty Amidst Plenty

The 1950s and 1960s were a period of growing prosperity. Family incomes were going up, and people were enjoying comfortable lives. This prosperity did not touch every American, however.

In 1959, the federal government said that an annual income of $2,973 was the poverty line. That meant a family of four earning less than that amount lived in poverty. The government found this number by figuring out how much it would cost a family of four to eat. Then that amount was multiplied by three—because people typically spent one-third of their income on food.

The graph below shows the percentage of families that earned different levels of income in 1959. As the graph shows, more than three-quarters of American families had incomes above the poverty line. Still, more than 22 percent of families did not.

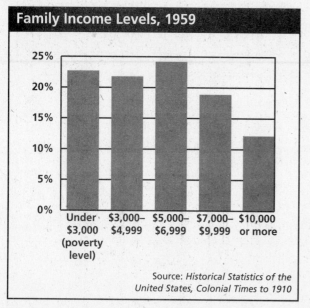

Family Income Levels, 1959

Source: *Historical Statistics of the United States, Colonial Times to 1910*

In the postwar boom times, people living in poverty were often overlooked. Social critic Michael Harrington brought them to the country's attention, however. In 1962, Harrington published a book called *The Other America*. It highlighted the problems of the poor. Harrington wrote the following.

The poor live in a culture of poverty. . . . The poor get sick more than anyone else in the society. . . . When they become sick, they are sick longer than any other group in the society. Because they are sick more often and longer than anyone else, they lose wages and work, and find it difficult to hold a steady job. . . . Their prospect is to move to an even lower level . . . toward even more suffering.

Harrington also pointed out the large numbers of poor people in the country. His book shocked many and spurred President John F. Kennedy to begin developing an antipoverty program. When Lyndon B. Johnson became president after President Kennedy's assassination in 1963, he vowed to end poverty. Saying that his goal was to create the Great Society, he sent Congress a number of antipoverty programs, which Congress passed. Some of the most important programs still exist.

- **Medicare** provides hospital and medical insurance for the elderly.
- **Medicaid** sends money to the states for health care for people receiving welfare.
- **Project Head Start** provides early education for poor children to prepare them better for school.

However, the Great Society had mixed success. The number of poor people did go down, and Project Head Start has been successful in preparing poor children for school. But several of the programs were ineffective. When the nation entered the Vietnam War in the mid-1960s, Congress spent less money on programs to fight poverty. Dr. Martin Luther King, Jr., said that the war on poverty was "shot down on the battlefields of Vietnam."

Activity

Find out what income is defined as the poverty level for a family of four today. Find out how many American families fall below that income.

The Debate over Affirmative Action

The term *affirmative action* stems from the executive order issued by President Lyndon Johnson on September 24, 1965, which required federal contractors "to take affirmative action to ensure that applicants are employed . . . without regard to their race, creed, color, or national origin." In the years following this directive, many state and local governments, as well as businesses and schools, created their own affirmative action programs in an effort to provide greater opportunities for minorities.

Over the years, affirmative action did indeed appear to provide an economic lift to people of color, including African Americans. According to the U.S. Census Bureau, for example, the percentage of the black labor force in white collar, or office, jobs rose from nearly 28 percent in 1970 to 38 percent in 1980. The percentage of African American men and women in management positions also increased—from 4 percent in 1970 to 18.6 percent in 1990 for men and from 2 percent to 13.3 percent for women. And while some private businesses showed little enthusiasm for affirmative action programs, others embraced such efforts. The affirmative action program at office-equipment maker Xerox, for instance, increased the company's percentage of minority workers from 3 percent to 27 percent between 1964 and 1996.

From almost their very inception, however, affirmative action programs have drawn criticism from people who feel that giving special treatment to minorities in the workplace or in the classroom is unfair and unconstitutional. Historians note that during the 1980s, the administration of President Ronald Reagan weakened numerous affirmative action initiatives. "We must not allow the noble concept of equal opportunity," declared Reagan, "to be distorted into federal guidelines or quotas which require race, ethnicity, or sex—rather than ability or qualifications—to be the principal factor in hiring or education."

The Supreme Court also curtailed affirmative action efforts with a number of rulings—including what many refer to as a landmark decision in the 1995 case, *Adarand Constructors* v. Pena. In this 5-to-4 ruling, the justices declared that federal affirmative action programs were permissible only if they "served a compelling governmental interest."

The ruling essentially called into question the constitutionality of affirmative action programs, and as a result the federal government began cutting back on its affirmative action measures. The Defense Department, for example, ended its practice of setting aside $1 billion worth of contracts for minority or women-owned firms.

In 2001, however, the justices refused to rule again on the case—which had made its way back to the Supreme Court after further argument in federal court. All of this has served only to intensify the debate over the constitutionality of affirmative action. In the years ahead, as minorities continue to try to improve their economic standing in society, the issue of whether or not they are entitled to special help will most likely remain a controversial topic.

Activity

Working with another student, use the Internet and other research tools to find the various Supreme Court cases addressing affirmative action in the 1970s, 1980s, and 1990s. Choose one of the cases and write a brief synopsis about it. Be sure to include the reason for the lawsuit as well as an explanation of the position the Court took. Present your report to the class.

Name _____ Date _____

Funding the War and Domestic Programs

As the war in Vietnam intensified, President Lyndon Johnson found himself facing dilemmas that were not only political and military in nature, but economic as well. By 1966, Johnson had become deeply involved in two gigantically expensive undertakings—the Vietnam War and the Great Society. The president was determined to pay for both his military and domestic endeavors, a practice commonly referred to as giving the country "guns and butter."

Johnson made his intent clear in his 1966 State of the Union address, when he declared that the United States was strong enough to fight communism abroad while fighting poverty at home. "Our Nation tonight is engaged in a brutal and bitter conflict in Vietnam," he stated. "But we will not permit those who fire upon us in Vietnam to win a victory over the desires and the intentions of all the American people. This nation is mighty enough, its society is healthy enough, its people are strong enough, to pursue our goals in the rest of the world while still building a Great Society here at home."

There was a catch to all this, however. Johnson sought to fully fund both the war and his domestic programs through increased deficit spending—and not through an income tax increase. The president wanted to avoid a tax hike in large part because he had just helped to push through a significant tax cut in 1964—which had played a key role in stimulating the country's economic growth. The president was not about to upset the flourishing economy with a tax hike.

His economic advisers, however, warned him that an increase in government spending eventually would pump too much money into the economy. This would lead to an increase in the demand for goods, which would drive up their prices and thus bring inflation.

This, of course, is exactly what happened. Between 1964 and 1969, the federal debt rose from about $316 billion to $367 billion. During those same years, the country's inflation rate jumped from 1.3 percent to 5.5 percent. By the end of 1967, a poll showed that 60 percent of Americans viewed the suddenly high cost of living as their number one concern. Only 5 percent voiced Vietnam as their number one worry.

That year, President Johnson finally sought a tax increase to help curb the country's spiraling inflation. The belief is that a tax hike works to bring down inflation by prompting people to spend less money. Such a drop in consumer demand tends to lower the price of goods.

The tax increase, however, appeared to be too little too late. A new set of economic woes visited the country in the 1970s—the most significant of which were continuous oil shortages—which boosted inflation even higher and pushed the country into a deep recession.

And while Lyndon Johnson was out of office by then, many analysts view his fiscal policies as an underlying cause of the economic downturn. They also point to his administration as a prime example of how difficult it is in the long run to fund both a war and a domestic agenda—or give the country guns and butter.

Activity

Small groups of students should choose several of their favorite items and create a chart or infographic tracking their rise in prices. In researching the inflationary history of their items, students should note any reasons or events that may have played a role in the price hikes. Students should present their visual to the class.

The Continuing Struggle of Migrant Workers

In the years since the farm workers movement of the 1960s, life for the men and women who toil on the nation's large farms has become one of hardship and despair—and the victories won by César Chávez and others but a distant a memory.

According to the Federal Commission on Agricultural Workers, the number of farm laborers rose from about 1.8 million to 2.5 million between 1960 and 1998. While once composed mainly of U.S. citizens, this workforce is now made up primarily of immigrants from Mexico and Central America. The increase in the migrant worker population countered the predictions made by agricultural experts in the 1960s that most crops eventually would be picked mechanically and that the migrant worker would become obsolete. The belief was that machines would be cheaper than farm workers—whose numerous labor gains during the 1960s and early 1970s had made them too costly to employers.

However, during the 1970s, many of the advances made on behalf of farm workers were rolled back. In California, for example, a string of pro-business governors relaxed the enforcement of the state's tough labor laws. Growers responded by firing farm workers who were union members and eliminating such hard-won benefits as sick leave, vacation pay, and health insurance. The use of migrant workers thus became so cheap that many of the machines developed for picking various fruits and vegetables never saw any use.

One of the main reasons that farm labor has become so inexpensive is that many of the workers—about 40 percent—are illegal immigrants, who lack both the means and desire to protest their poor working conditions. "Employers avoid incredible hassles by bringing in [illegal] immigrants," notes one expert on the topic. "They can get immigrants to work terribly hard under supervision that Americans would resent or resist."

While the country's more than 2 million migrant workers perform jobs that few Americans want—and help fuel the nation's agricultural economy in the process—they are by no means well compensated. Farm laborers are the lowest paid and least protected workers in America. Despite the establishment of a minimum wage in 1938, agricultural workers were not covered by the wage minimum until 1966—and even then it was set lower than that of other workers. During the mid-1990s, the average migrant worker earned only about $5,000.

In addition to the other benefits they are denied, many farm workers lack adequate housing. In 1998, about 800,000 workers had no adequate shelter, according to the Housing Assistance Council, a Washington, D.C.-based organization that studies rural housing. These workers were forced to sleep in such places as trailers, garages, and even outside in parks or forest preserves. In 1998, the federal government spent $27.5 million to help provide more housing for farm laborers—far less than the $69 million spent in 1979.

Nearly forty years after the future looked so bright for farm workers, most are now trapped in a life of poverty and poor working conditions—even as they play what many would acknowledge is a significant role in the nation's farming economy.

Activity

Small groups of students should choose a state and research its history of migrant labor from the past to the present. The groups should then present a multimedia presentation of the information it found, using photographs, charts or graphs, and an oral narrative.

Name _____   Date _____

Inflation Eats Away at the Dollar

During the 1970s, prices went up. This inflation had begun in the late 1960s, when spending by the federal government rose. Great Society programs and the war in Vietnam were expensive. President Johnson did not want to anger voters by raising taxes. As a result, the government had to borrow the money. This borrowing put more money into the economy. At the same time, the economy slumped. Businesses were producing less and less. The combination of more money and fewer goods pushed prices up.

In the middle 1970s, inflation rose even more sharply. Rising oil prices sent inflation soaring more than ten percent a year.

The table shows the effect that inflation had on some common goods.

Activity

Find the prices today of the five foods listed in the chart. Be sure to find prices using the same measure as in the chart (per pound, per dozen, and so on). Make a chart comparing those prices to the 1977 prices. Then calculate how much prices have gone up—or down—since 1977. Has inflation continued at the same high rate as in the 1970s? Remember that the chart here shows price increases over a seven-year period. Your comparison will be over many more years.

Item	1970	1971	1972	1973	1974	1975	1976	1977	Increase*
Foods									
apples (per pound)	$0.25	$0.27	$0.27	$0.32	$0.38	$0.36	$0.36	$0.42	68%
eggs (per dozen)	$0.67	$0.58	$0.57	$0.84	$0.86	$0.85	$0.91	$0.89	33%
potatoes (10 pound bag)	$0.94	$0.94	$1.00	$1.47	$1.76	$1.41	$1.61	$1.67	78%
rice (per pound)	$0.22	$0.24	$0.24	$0.30	$0.51	$0.50	$0.48	$0.45	105%
round steak (per pound)	$1.54	$1.64	$1.78	$2.02	$2.12	$2.25	$2.12	$2.10	36%
Other Goods									
bicycle	$44.00	$44.00	$44.00	$56.00	$79.00	$75.00	$80.00	$84.00	91%
diapers	$2.57	$2.57	$1.95	$2.87	$2.49	$3.77	$3.99	$3.99	55%
flashlight battery	$0.21	$0.21	$0.26	$0.31	N/a	$0.35	$0.29	$0.40	90%
sewing machine	$89.00	$79.00	$90.00	$90.00	$82.00	$77.00	$112.00	$116.00	30%
stereo	$120.00	$200.00	$170.00	$155.00	N/a	$178.00	$230.00	$190.00	58%

Data are for New York City
*Increase from 1970 to 1977.
N/a—Information not available

Reaganomics

Ronald Reagan campaigned for president in 1980 vowing to make major changes in how the federal government acted. He had plans to change how much the government spent and how much it collected in taxes. His economics program came to be called "Reaganomics."

Every year from 1969 to 1980, the government spent more money than it collected. The extra money had to be borrowed. The federal debt—all the money that the federal government owed—grew larger every year. By the 1980 election, the government owed $709.3 billion. Reagan said this hurt the economy because investors were loaning money to the government rather than to businesses. This slowed the growth of the economy.

Reagan wanted to make deep cuts in education, welfare, and similar programs. The Democrats controlled the House of Representatives. They made cuts in domestic programs, but not as many as Reagan wanted. At the same time, Reagan rapidly increased defense spending. As a result, overall government spending continued to grow.

Reagan also wanted to cut taxes. He said that people would spend or invest the money they saved. This investment would help fuel business growth, which would lower unemployment. In the end, the government would collect more taxes as a result of this economic growth.

Taxes were cut; between 1981 and 1983, they were lowered by 25 percent. And the economy did grow. However, that growth was not as fast as Reagan had hoped. Government revenues did not increase as much as expected. This, combined with the higher levels of federal spending, produced even bigger budget deficits.

Reagan was President from 1981 to 1989. During this period, the government had to borrow between $121 billion and almost $180 billion each year. The result can be seen in the graph below. The federal debt soared between 1981 and 1989. By 1990, the government owed nearly $2.5 trillion.

At the same time, though, the economy grew during most of Reagan's presidency. Partly because of lower taxes, consumers had more money to spend—and they spent it. Unemployment fell as companies hired workers. And the inflation of the 1970s was no longer a problem.

Yet the federal budget deficit continued to grow because the federal government did not collect enough taxes. The deficit continued to be a major issue into the 1990s. It was a major issue in the 1992 election, helping third-party candidate H. Ross Perot to win almost 20 percent of the vote. In 1997, though, President Bill Clinton and Congress agreed on budget cuts. In 1998, for the first time since the 1960s, the government had a surplus.

Activity

Find out about the federal debt today. Find out how much money the federal government owed in five recent years. Is that number going up or down? Why? What policies in Washington are making it change?

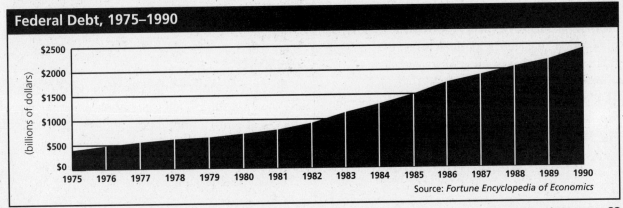

Federal Debt, 1975–1990

(billions of dollars)

Source: *Fortune Encyclopedia of Economics*

The New Economy

What exactly is meant by the "new economy"? Economists characterize it as a combination of two main trends over the past decade or so. The first is the revolution in information technology. The invention of the microprocessor—which made possible the development of the computer, fax machine, and cell phone—has dramatically changed the way Americans live and work. While the manufacturing of goods once drove the nation's economy, it is now the delivery of information and services—with the help of these modern communication tools—that fuels the country's economic engine. By the mid-1990s, nearly 80 percent of all jobs in the United States resided in the service sector. Information technology accounted for a quarter to a third of the nation's economic growth.

The second aspect of the new economy is the globalization of business. From e-mails to fax machines, wireless technology has made doing business with foreign companies as easy as if they were located down the block. In addition, a number of recent international agreements have lowered trade barriers among many countries of the world. The result of all this for the United States and other nations is an increase in international commerce. While imports and exports made up 17 percent of the U.S. economy in the late 1970s, for example, they now account for about 25 percent.

Few would disagree that this "new" economy has been a good one for America, as it ushered in the longest economic expansion in U.S. history—from 1991 to 2001. During this decade-long boom, the overall economy expanded, the stock market soared, and unemployment reached its lowest levels in decades. One reason for the low rate of joblessness was the creation of so many information-related jobs. Between 1980 and 1997—as the country shifted from a manufacturing to a service economy—43 million jobs were lost but 71 million new ones created.

Also contributing to the economic growth of the 1990s was a steady rise in worker productivity— prompted in large part by the extensive use of technology. As workers in nearly every field used computers to help them perform their jobs more quickly and easily, worker productivity rose a healthy 3 percent each year between 1995 and 2000.

Globalization played a role in the economic boom as well. The increase in global trade, first and foremost, opened new markets for U.S. goods and services. In addition, as trade barriers fell, cheaper goods became more available around the world—including in the United States.

To be sure, the new economy has not been beneficial for everyone. Most of today's information-related jobs require a higher degree of skill than the jobs of the past. As a result, many unskilled laborers have had trouble finding work or earning a decent living. In addition, the increase in globalization has prompted a number of U.S. companies to move overseas—mainly for cheaper labor—leaving scores of American workers unemployed.

And for all its strength, the new economy was not immune to a recession. According to the country's leading economists, the U.S. economy fell into a recession in March of 2001. A recession is an economic downturn marked by at least six months of declining gross domestic product. The economy took a further hit in September of 2001 when the terrorist attacks on the World Trade Center crippled the airline industry and many industries related to it. Like the others before it, however, this recession will be temporary. The new economy, on the other hand, is most likely here to stay.

Activity

Choose a modern communication device, such as the Internet, e-mail, cell phone, fax machine, etc., and write a brief report about how it has impacted the way Americans do business. Use the appropriate library resources to help you conduct research into your topic.

Answer Key

The Benefits of Trade
Students' lists of goods that come from other countries are likely to include such consumer items as automobiles, televisions, VCRs, clothing, cameras, bicycles, and so forth. Japan, China, and Mexico are countries that are likely to turn up on many lists.

Farming in the English Colonies
Students should mention soil conservation; new and sophisticated farm machinery; economies of scale in farming huge plots of land with state-of-the-art technology; new hybrids and varieties of crops that stand up well to pests and difficult climate conditions; newer, safer, and more efficient pesticides; more sophisticated weather information.

Mercantilism and Colonies
Students might suggest a number of measure to discourage colonies from trading with other countries. For example, they might suggest a special tax or surcharge on goods produced in the colonies that are traded with any country other than the home country. Or students might suggest legislation to discourage colonial trade with any country other than the home country. Of course, the colonists would be likely to resent any such legislation or taxation as interference from the home country.

The Impact of British Taxes
Students might come up with a number of different ideas to raise money to keep troops in North America. They might suggest a lottery in which the money not distributed in prizes would go for the support of troops, much as today money that flows into state coffers through lotteries is often earmarked for educational needs. Or students might suggest different taxes, such as a general sales tax rather than taxes on specific items. Property taxes and inheritance taxes might be other possibilities.

The Value of Land
Reports prepared by students will vary depending upon the kind of area in which they live. City, suburban, and rural areas all face different issues. Overcrowding and overdevelopment, for example, are more likely to be an issue in the suburbs; rural areas are more likely to be concerned with lack of development. Local issues should be reflected in the students' reports.

Personal Banking
Students should, if possible, visit a variety of banks in the area to get an idea of the different kinds of accounts that are available. Students should find out about minimum-balance requirements for checking accounts and whether or not this affects the fee charged for the account. Students should find out if they can set up an account on their own, or if a parent needs to also sign for the account. Students might collect brochures at the bank they visit which describe the various accounts in detail and use these brochures as part of a report or display.

The Economics of Slavery
Students may or may not agree that slavery did not make economic sense. Both sides of the issue have been argued by scholars, although the majority feel that slavery hurt the South's economy. Accept any reasonable response from students that is supported by evidence.

Growth of the Factory System
Student reports will vary, but should show evidence of adequate research. Written reports should include such information as how much product the factory produces each year and how many workers it employees, as well as when and why it opened. Visual presentations should provide a detailed depiction of how the factory's product is made.

Gold Rush Entrepreneurs
You might have students design posters that advertise their new businesses. Then choose an area in the classroom and allow students to display their posters. Their posters, and businesses, might address trends in entertainment, health care, exercise, sports, education, television, music, movies, and so on.

Irish Immigration
In the nineteenth century, most immigrants came from Europe. Today, most immigrants come from Asia, North America (Mexico), and Central America. According to the U. S. Bureau of the Census, between 1981–1996 most of the immigrants to this country came from Mexico, the Philippines, Vietnam, China, Dominican Republic, India, Korea, Soviet Union (the former Soviet Republics), El Salvador, and Poland.

The Value of the Border States
Provide an area in the classroom for students to display their posters. Make sure that each of the major regions of the country is represented. You may wish to assign regions to make sure that students do not all choose their own region. An encyclopedia would provide a

Answer Key

great deal of information about each region, including economic activities in that area.

Understanding the Business Cycle

This topic might be easier for students to understand if they focus on the Chairman of the Federal Reserve Board. Students should be able to find information about the chairman and the Federal Reserve in a variety of sources available in the library as well as on the Internet. Point out to students that the Fed raises interest rates by small increments in order to keep a lid on inflation.

The Law of Supply and Demand

Most students will probably think that if a professional athlete is the best player at a particular position, then he is unique or one-of-a-kind and his value is higher. There will be increased competition for such a player's services. Consequently, such an athlete's salary demands will be higher.

The Union Struggle

Students might start by looking up the entry on unions in an encyclopedia or on the Internet. The union movement is weaker today than it was in the 1950s or 1960s. A smaller percentage of the workforce belongs to unions today than in the past. Nonetheless, certain unions, such as the United Auto Workers and the Teamsters, still have large memberships and considerable political influence.

Conflict over Tariffs

Student responses will vary. Students should state their position clearly and support their position with documented facts and evidence. Invite volunteers to share their paragraphs with the rest of the class.

The Rise of Department Stores

Most cities have at least one department store that offers a variety of goods and services under one roof. Marshall Field's in Chicago, Bloomingdale's in New York, and Neiman Marcus in Dallas are among the more famous department stores that students might study. Increasingly, department stores find themselves in competition with mail-order marketing, shopping malls, specialty stores, and the Internet.

Tariffs and Taxes

Students should be able to discover through encyclo-pedia articles, almanacs, the Internet, and other sources that most of the revenues for the federal government come from the income tax. State and local govern-ments get their money from various combinations of income, sales, and property taxes.

The Economic Causes of Imperialism

You might ask students who researched the same countries to do group reports of their findings. In addition, they could present their findings in charts that show the types of products that the two countries trade. The United States has trading relationships with all the nations except Cuba. The U.S. has a trade boycott with Cuba because of its Communist government.

Russian Communism

Students should include in their reports some indication of the present status of the Communist regime in each country. In some of the countries mentioned, Communist ideology remains rigid and inflexible. Others, particularly China, have moved toward a free-market economy. All of the countries in Eastern Europe have overthrown Communism.

Understanding the Stock Market

The Dow Jones industrial average is based upon the performance of 30 stocks. In October of 1999, four of these stocks changed. Sears was dropped from the list of 30 stocks, as were Chevron, Goodyear, and Union Carbide. Microsoft was added to the list of 30 stocks, along with Intel, SBC Communications, and Home Depot.

Women's Economic Impact

Reports should be well organized with a topic sentence and supporting details and should show evidence of adequate research. Encourage students to research areas where women have made significant strides as well as those where advancement has been more difficult. Students should include graphs or charts in their reports to better illustrate their findings.

The Great Depression

You might wish to assign certain countries to make sure that each region and continent is represented. This will help students to understand that the Great Depression had an impact on countries in South America and Asia as well as in Europe.

Deficit Spending

Student reports will vary, but should show evidence of adequate research. Written reports should include such

Answer Key

information as causes of the deficits and debt as well as any actions taken to make up the shortfalls. Visual presentations should provide a detailed depiction of the trends of both the deficits and the debt. After students have presented their reports, lead a class discussion about the overall impact of deficits and debt on the nation's economy.

The Lend-Lease Act

Reports will vary. Each one should be well organized and show clear evidence of adequate research. Interested students might form teams and stage a class debate, using their research and quotations as the basis for their presentations.

The Growing Economic Role of Government

Set aside an area in the classroom where students can display their pie graphs. Information to complete the pie graph may be found in almanacs and annual government publications such as the *Statistical Abstract of the United States: The National Data Book,* published annually by the U. S. Bureau of the Census.

The Space Race Pays Off

Students whose primary concern is the free flow of information might support the policy of making the Landsat images available to people all over the world. Students whose primary concern is national security may oppose such a policy. Based on the essays that students have written, you might choose to stage a debate between those on either side of the issue. Those students who write the best essays for or against the policy might be chosen as the members of the two teams.

Measuring the Postwar Boom

The American economy over the last ten years has shown remarkable strength. This vitality is reflected in GNP and median family income. After students have made their graphs, lead a class discussion of the possible meaning of these economic measures.

Poverty Amidst Plenty

The poverty level changes annually. Information about the poverty level for a family of four can be obtained on the Internet, in almanacs that are widely available in the library, as well as in government publications such as *Current Population Reports,* published by the Bureau of the Census (part of the U. S. Department of Commerce).

The Debate over Affirmative Action

Student responses will vary, depending on which case they choose to research. Students should state their position clearly and support their position with documented facts and evidence. Help students get started on their research by providing various print sources and Internet sites related to Supreme Court cases.

Funding the War and Domestic Programs

Encourage students to use a variety of formats for their charts or infographics. Remind students that infographics can include diagrams and images as well as charts or graphs. Student's presentations should be well organized and show clear evidence of adequate research.

The Continuing Struggle of Migrant Workers

Student reports will vary. Each one should be well organized and show clear evidence of adequate research. Student presentations will likely focus on states with the highest number of migrant workers, including California, Texas and Florida. Their presentations should also include mention of the three major streams of migrant worker movements from the 1960s to the present: the Pacific Coast, the MidWest, and the Atlantic Coast.

Inflation Eats Away at the Dollar

Prices today for the five foods listed will be higher than they were in the 1970s. However, students will undoubtedly discover that the rate of inflation was much lower in the 1990s than it was in the 1970s. Although prices are higher for these items now than they were in 1977 (the last year on the chart), they are lower than they would be if the 1970s rate of inflation had continued through the 1990s.

Reaganomics

Students will discover that, for the first time in years, the federal debt is slowly being paid down. Students may disagree whether this is the result of specific government actions or the result of an expanding and unusually strong economy.

The New Economy

Student reports will vary. Each one should be well organized and show clear evidence of adequate research. Students who select the Internet as their topic should cite specific businesses that have developed and explain how and why they have succeeded.